SHALL WE DANCE?

ALSO BY SUSAN K. HAGEN

Allegorical Remembrance: A Study of The Life of the Pilgrimage of Man *as a Medieval Treatise on Seeing and Remembering*, University of Georgia Press, 1990.

SHALL WE DANCE?

Poems of Desire and Meditation

Susan K. Hagen

Antrim House
Bloomfield, Connecticut

Copyright © 2021 by Susan K. Hagen

Except for short selections reprinted for purposes of
book review, all reproduction rights are reserved.
Requests for permission to replicate should
be addressed to the publisher.

Library of Congress Control Number: 2021907566

ISBN: 978-1-943826-83-4

First Edition, 2021

Printed & bound by Ingram Content Group

Book design by Rennie McQuilkin

Front cover photograph by the author

Author photograph by Brenda Bailey

Antrim House
860.217.0023
AntrimHouseBooks@gmail.com
www.AntrimHouseBooks.com
400 Seabury Dr., #5196, Bloomfield, CT 06002

For Georgann,
who lovingly creates, protects, and fosters
the space for me to create.

Acknowledgements

"To the Least of These" first appeared in the online publication, *The Weekly Avocet #336,* 8 December 2019.

"The Art of Exultation," "The Fool" (under the title "Simplicity"), and an earlier version of Part II of "Garden Penitential" (under the title "The Good Gardener") appeared in my personal blog, *After Eden,* in 2017.

Special appreciation is due to James Wren and Dunya Habash for their reading, reviewing, prompting—even prodding—on behalf of these poems. I also want to thank my patient readers over the past two years: GK Armstrong, Whitney Williams, and Michael Yusko. One might write in isolation but never grow as a writer. Thanks, too, to Sandra Sprayberry for early coaching and to Dan Slone, who first planted thoughts of publication in my mind. Finally, to Rosie who ever reminds me of my place in the scheme of things.

Table of Contents

A Prologue / 3

After Reading Hafiz / 5
The Starlight Room / 6
Sensuality of Spirit / 7
Most Vulnerable / 8
Commemoration / 9
Evening Intimate / 10
Love's Music / 11
Limitations / 12
Beauty in Ugly Fruit / 13
Seasons / 14
Kiss of the Spirit / 15
The Play of Energy and Ego / 16
Gethsemane / 17
Struggle / 18
To the Least of These / 19
Silenced by Solemnity / 20
Weight of Myself / 21
All That Is / 22
Thoughts of the Belovèd / 23
An Allegory of Religion   / 24
March 2020 / 26
30 May 2020 / 27
Lectio Divina / 28
Garden Penitential / 29
Smoke Rising / 31
Bunting / 32
While Sitting by the Window… / 33
Wind Carrying Spray / 34

Exegesis / 35
Of Mystics / 36
Icon / 37
Corona / 38
Meditation 1 / 39
Meditation 2 / 40
Meditation 3 / 41
Meditation 4 / 42
True Subjunctive / 43
Love's Acrobatics / 44
One Afternoon / 45
The Fool / 46
Pentimento / 47
Fossil / 48
Ruffner Mountain / 49
Marjana Woman's Co-Operative,
   Morocco / 50
Someday / 51
World Heritage / 52
The House of Mary / 53
Mirrored / 54
Shall We Dance? / 55

About the Author / 57
About the Book / 58

They who dance are thought mad by those who hear not the music. – author uncertain

SHALL WE DANCE?

A Prologue

As I approached retirement after decades of undergraduate teaching and scholarly research in medieval literature, people would ask me, "What will you do now?"

The Art of Exultation

What will you do now that your work is done?
I will sing the song I have not yet sung.

I will sing a song with words that have never been said,
Invoking images that have never been imagined.
Songs that will make Solomon feel new canticles of desire
And the Daughters of Jerusalem chant new choruses of love.

I will play harmonies that have never before been heard,
So compelling, attending stars in their circuits will pause to listen.
Half the world will see their hesitation, wondering at the halting
of the heavens;
Half the world will suspect that they have missed some
mystic revelation.

I will dance a dance with steps impossible for human feet
With abandoned enthusiasm that outpaces David before God's ark,
With leaps and twirls and timing terrifying to conceive,
With movements incredible of power, strength, and grace.
I will sing of you and me, and the pulse of all creation,

Of all that barks and buzzes, of all that floats and flies,
Of all that fruits and flourishes, of all that wants and waits.
I will sing, and play, and dance in exultation. But,

Until my song is sung, my work will not be done.

After Reading Hafiz

Bernini's St. Teresa comes the closest in Western art,
closest to the ecstasy of desire fulfilled by the divine,
closest to admitting the sensuality of spirit,
closest to the complete abandonment of the body
to the experience of the Belovèd.

Oh, Herbert tried. And Donne knew the body
was kin to the spirit,
but prayed to be battered rather than beloved.

Yet, passion is passion. Desire is desire.
Longing so intense that it hollows the body,
stops the mind, and burns the heart is longing.

To be fair, 15th-century Anonymous knew—
knew that the language of courtly longing
could capture the Christ's passion
even before the Passion.

A hundred years before, Julian found
mother and brother in the universal Love,
speaking in homely conversation,
assured that all shall be well,

while her Eastern brother Hafiz
celebrated the kinship
of sensuality and spirit.

The Starlight Room

three-quarter spotlight moon
sequined sky
night-creature continuo—
why are we not making love
with Ginger Rogers elegance?

Sensuality of Spirit

In a book with the words of
Rabia, Francis, Hafiz, Catherine
filled with
the sensuality of spirit,
celebration of creation,
simplicity of soul,
devotion of desire,

I keep a bookmark—
da Vinci's *Leda and the Swan,*
      the curvature of her thigh softly
      enfolded
      in his feathery wing—
Perfect.
The nesting of the beloved in the
body of the Belovèd.

Most Vulnerable

Loving ignited by desire in the eye
inflames a great passion of living.
Loving kindled by searching lips and sweet kisses
warms in the ease of familiarity.

But in the turquoise-blue hours before sunrise,
when my lover wakes me
with soft pressure on my shoulder,
pulling me closer,
eyes entreating,
lips unmoving in silent appeal,
love is most vulnerable,
most wanted, most proffered,
most beloved.

Commemoration

Sometime when sleeping,
my legs intertwined with those of my lover,
I dream of previous pleasures—
another's hand soft on my shoulder,
another's lips breathing desire upon my neck,
another's body forming the harbor of my refuge.

Awake, guilt follows me,
an old aroma of holidays
long gone by.

On jubilee nights, though,
all my lovers gather,
a chorus guiltless, singing a prologue to the
unimaginable sensuality of the Belovèd.

Evening Intimate

Sometimes I fear the night—
the dread of slipping into bed alone,
my sole companion anxious expectation
of haunts of loss and hurt.

Sometimes, though, the Belovèd comes quietly
to breathe a soft blanket over me
and pull it up over my shoulders
so that dread might not touch me.

Why do I not invite the Belovèd to my bed
more often?

Love's Music

When I think of my lover,
I become a hundred harp strings
trembling for the touch of her hand.

When I think of the Belovèd,
I am a mountain of treetops
caressed by the wind's
love-song of creation.

Limitations

You have done it to me again,
    my sweet one,
your honeyed tongue fashioning promise
    out of darker portend.

Do I endure the dulling ache
    of your forgetfulness
for the hope of soft kisses
    upon my cheek?
Or do I secretly welcome
    the seduction of self-delusion?

I should better trust
    the wind's kiss upon my cheek
    and wisdom's whisper in my ear.

Beauty in Ugly Fruit

Almost all the pears have fallen
hard on the deck,
smashing speckled yellow-green skins—
pear sauce for pinching black ants,
prison-striped yellow jackets,
big bottomed bumble bees,
an occasional red-spotted purple—
pears with brown-edged gouges
from penetrating crow beaks,
with squirrel bites
on rounded tear-drop sides,
all rotting into sticky, bug-intoxicating juiciness.
Remembrance of summer,
dark pulpy stain on wood.

Seasons

solstice geometries
dark threshold of spring
bright axis rising
old lines falling away—
the empty space in the body's curve

Kiss of the Spirit

Some say a strong wind
    is a cruel wind.
The Belovèd says
    it is the kiss of the spirit
    desirous for creation.

The Play of Energy and Ego

From my window seat,
the garden becomes stage
to hunger and greed,
birds rushing refilled feeders.

Cardinals, red-feathered males and red-beaked females,
chase black-capped chickadees and sparrows.
Hummingbirds, red-throated and turquoise,
fend each other off like flying spears,
in favor of drinking from the feeder,
nectar left abandoned to the bees.

A woodpecker flings seeds hastily to the ground,
intent on the one nut in the light summer blend.
A Carolina wren chases, captures, devours a fat spider,
cleaning his beak side to side
on a branch of the pear tree.

A chipmunk, thought victim of the neighbors' cat,
returns to join the feeding,
filling his cheeks with woodpecker castoff,
running off to empty his hoard in some new
cat-free space.

Overwhelmed by the play of energy and ego,
caught between inferences of necessity and cruelty,
I turn to the Belovèd, who breathes,
    "I, too, see it in my Garden."

Gethsemane

Feeling alone,
I sat in the garden crying
until the breath of
the Belovèd dried my tears
whispering, "I understand."

Struggle

How easily I find the Belovèd in my garden.
Bloom, butterfly, bird and bug,
all embroider the garment of universal Love.
Even in the eyes of my dog,
who dares to look me directly,
deeply, in the eye
or in the soft eye of horse or otter or other,
I find the probing spirit of the Belovèd.

But on the morning streets, in the underground,
in the rush of work and worry
where human eyes grow pale and averting
and I am not moved
to touch, or pet, or embrace,
where I must face how threadbare—
how worn and warped—
the garment of universal Love can be,
I struggle to find the Belovèd, who
still with eyes averted
looks back at me.

To the Least of These

The shade of weathered wood,
from a distance down the road
a thick twig
or short stick, an uplifted crick on the end.

But, in turtle season
warm asphalt and impelling desire call
for crossing to the other side,
seductive reptile mystery on country roads.

I named it before I passed,
stretched neck and upturned head
body raised on short in-turned legs—
slow motion frozen in turtle-indecision.

Skirting wide to avoid, to give space
on the morning road,
I could not avoid my own reproach.

I did not stop.
I did not carry it to the other side.

For a mile or two
saying *it will be safe*,
saying *there is no place to turn around*,
my better self followed close behind.

Turning back, driving slowly,
searching where the margin met the road
there was no short stick, no twig, no turtle—
only a suspicion of a testing of the Spirit.

Silenced by Solemnity

Sometimes I am silenced
by the solemnity of prayer.
Then the Belovèd touches my cheek
And asks, "Can we just talk?"

Weight of Myself

Kneeling by the single candle,
bent forward under the weight
of myself,
I admitted, "I have not treated you well.
Have not kept my promises.
Have not always been kind."

"I know.
I know,"
imparted the Belovèd as faintly
as candlelight.
"Yet, I confess I can
love you none the less."

All That Is

Dahlia petal-fingers
unfurling reveal
all that is,
        held
in the palm of the Belovèd.

Thoughts of the Belovèd

Sometimes in the garden
when contemplating the Belovèd,
my attention wanders—
        hummingbirds sound like tiny propellers
        molting cardinals lack bright mating plumage
        naïve chipmunks recklessly burrow where
            the cat hides among stalks of Obedient Plants
        roses need pruning
        few Rose of Sharon blooms remain
        tight anemone buds relax in pre-bloom.
I rebuke myself,
struggle to return to thoughts of the Belovèd,
and hear,
"Be at ease. You did not lose your way."

An Allegory of Religion

In a time not long after time, three pious seekers of Illumination and Peace came upon a sparkling spring in a verdant glade.

The water glistened in the sun.

The air carried its cool mists and melodic sounds and bore the aroma of spice trees and blossoms.

The ground wore a blanket of thick emerald moss as soft as the most precious of silk rugs.

The seekers fell to their knees and declared, "We have discovered Peace. We must share it with the people!"

One then advised, "We must first build a wall to protect the spring from wild animals."

The second cautioned, "We must build a pavilion to protect the spring from falling limbs and strong winds."

Finally, the third counseled, "We must build paths so that the people do not misstep before the spring."

So, they built a shining wall of the finest stone around the entire glade.

They erected a splendid pavilion over the spring and decorated it with hammered gold.

They laid down wide footpaths of the rarest marble leading to and past the spring.

When all was readied, they journeyed throughout the land, telling the people about Peace being found at the spring.

And the people came.

Respectfully and expectantly, they entered within the wall through massive gates of magnificently carved oak, hinged with expertly wrought iron.

They moved with ordered and metered steps to the spring, through the pavilion, and past the spring. The spring, though, surrounded now by cold stone and shielded from the sky and trees, ran less joyfully and sparkled less brightly for lack of sunshine and aromatic breezes.

Anxious for their approbation, the three spiritual seekers asked the people exiting the glade, "Did you find Peace?"

The people said that they found beauty and order in abundance, but that Peace was nowhere to be found.

March 2020

In the light of candles,
and the smoke of incense,
with the sound of bells ringing to silence,
and the taste of mortality in their mouths,
they assumed the posture of supplication,
and prayed.

"Belovèd, Belovèd,
do you not see our pain?
Do you not feel our fear?
When will you relieve our dread
and take this trial from us?"

And the breath of the Belovèd
fell upon their shoulders,
"Relief has always been within you
as you are within the Belovèd."

30 May 2020

From the depth of human innocence,
from the height of human temerity,
I challenged the Belovèd,

"You are all compassionate.
You are all merciful.
Why do you let us suffer poverty, disease, violence?"

Heaven did not darken.
Thunder did not roll.

A sweet breeze only
answered me, enfolded me,
whispering,
"How else would you learn
compassion and mercy?"

Lectio Divina

I've studied your library.
Your languages, lessons,
parables and stories.
Your fathers and mothers,
their children, their crimes
and their triumphs.
Warnings and wisdom,
and wonders of your glory.
Your justice and mercy,
your power and beauty.

But my friend died today.

Proffer me no stories.
Be by my side.

Garden Penitential

I

I often bleed in the garden.
Intent on clearing the dead and uninvited,
not heeding the thorns of wild blackberry or rose,
spines pierce and scratch unnoticed.

Catbrier and Greenbrier,
with arrow and heart-shaped leaves,
their thread-thin stems the strength of steel
defy extraction.

Pale tubers deep within dark ground hold fast,
sacrifice stem-snap at the surface
to remain untouched at heart
to sprout and spool and twist and rasp
ascending again into light uninvited.

II

For healthy trees—

Cut out the dead
    wood,
branches damaged
    by frost or storm.
Eliminate the crossing limbs
    that rub bark raw and
    defenseless to disease.

Keep the center open
      for air and sun.
By-pass pruners
      sharpened,
make cuts clean,
          angled slightly
at the stem collar
      for better healing.

III

At Nature's mercy
the work of hand, shovel, and shears—
alms owed to creation.

Smoke Rising

In the gray of morning just before the
orange-red rising of the sun,
I put a flame to incense,
breathe gently on the ember glow,
watch bluish smoke rise,
a spiraling image of gratefulness
and supplication,
dispersing into air.
Gaze falling
from floating,
fading smoke
lifting the fragrance
of myrrh and mystics,
I look from my window
to find the Belovèd
sitting in the garden
waiting for me.

Bunting

Color between midnight
   and the blue-hour before sunrise
flash of indigo through
   crepe myrtle
shadowed black at rest

Migratory wings
   carrying compulsion and persistence
teasing out an answer to my question
   posed to the garden through the window

While Sitting by the Window
Googling Thomas Merton's "the true life"

Two mourning doves with slight sideways gaits
marched right outside the window
   one before the other
close enough to see
   the pinkish-brown iridescence of their necks,
near enough to chart the change
   from daybreak gray to buff on their bodies,
to count the charcoal spots on their wings,
heads thrusting forward and
   back with the rhythm of their steps
as though pointing the way to some dove-desired destination.

With military precision they turned,
   follower to leader
   leader to follower,
and exited stage right.

Wind Carrying Spray

Standing on the cliffs
wary I was of the wind
carrying spray
from the ocean below
until I realized
wind and spray were
the breath of the Belovèd
and a baptism into creation.

Exegesis

It is important, you know,
   to weed your garden.
But it is more important
   to be able to recognize the weeds.

An aphorism, you say,
   common place and mundane.
No.
A parable
   filled with every enigma
   that is the Belovèd.

Of Mystics

Walking through a gray-green wooded area
high forest canopy of red oak and pine
understory of oakleaf and maple leaf viburnum
cone-shaped and flat-top flowers
whispering white in the deep-green,

the Belovèd and I emerged in a clearing
heaven-high canopy of clouds
underfoot clover and wild daises
small globes and heliocentric flowers
shouting white in the lemon-yellow light.

I asked the Belovèd, "What do you think of mystics?"
The Belovèd said, "Some things bloom in the gray-green;
some things bloom in the heat of pure light."

Icon

They will not
      look you in the eyes.

Over your right shoulder
slightly above your head
something there is
        askance
to their left, or
          hovering behind,
beyond, before, or after you
that holds their attention.

Perception without expression,
      unchanging lips neither
    smile nor frown,
        frozen
in the invisible, impossible, ineffable
    pull outside of you.

They will not
      look you in the eyes.
You cannot follow
      their gaze—
          only guess.

Corona

Have I become
a recluse,
a religious,
engaging others
through the cell window
of a computer screen,
embroidering altar linen
with plant descriptions
and photography,
the crown of it all
willful distance—
freeing time
clearing space
for connecting
with everything?

Meditation 1

Neither anointed nor appointed,
how could she come from heaven
bringing with her only opened hands?

Meditation 2

How hard it is
to embrace the difference
between need and desire!

Need fills
the heart's fearful void.
Desire yearns
for the passionate
conflagration
of the entire self into
ash—
to re-form, remade,
refined.

Belovèd,
      Oh, Belovèd,
bring the fire.

Meditation 3

Mercy I understand—
leniency beyond deserving,
compassion beyond expectation,
transgression repaid with forgiveness.

There are equivalencies,
actions considered,
debts weighed and balanced.

Grace, though,
like an expanding universe,
I cannot grasp.

No cognitive context,
no image to illustrate,
no icon to place in memory
or on the wall.

Not earned,
maybe not even desired,
simply willed upon us.

Meditation 4

When we say, "I pray for—"
What is it we seek?
Justice from our leaders,
security for the impoverished,
comfort for the troubled
      in body, mind, or spirit,
peace with our enemies,
wise use of Your creation?

Putting this all in your hands, Belovèd,
What, then, do we offer in return?

True Subjunctive

Were I to meet a demon
face-to-face,
would I be steadfast,
Belovèd?

"Of course.
Were you to meet a demon
face-to-face,
you would know,
I am
   not imaginary."

Love's Acrobatics

A blood-red, feathered spot,
barely a finger-sized smear on the nape,
catches the eye in rhythmic alternation—
visible, hidden, visible.

Turning, head cocked—left, right, left—
the Downy Woodpecker
judges, calculates, gauges
distance from tree limb
to the last chunk of fatty cake
lodged in the suet cage
hung from a branch above.

Rotating his body,
spot down, beak up,
he stretches his neck,
as if in inverted song,
to reach and grasp his prize.

One Afternoon in November

a flash of light
along the road—

Entering the room
to 60s radio playing,
I saw you before you were mine.
Tenderness overwhelmed me,
your teenage self
emerging from the body
I've come to know so well,
someone unknown,
freshly familiar.

Belovèd, not all epiphanies
are conversions.
Are some not confirmations?

The Fool

Let me dance with St. Francis
naked-faced in the streets of the city

Find the beacon of the pole star
and fly in formation with migrating wings

Laugh with the dolphin
and swim with joy in the sea

Hear the unseen cicada
and welcome the coming of night

Sway with the bent pine in the howling wind
and dig my hands in the earth next to sprawling rose roots

Extend my hand to take the paw of the wolf
and sing with her in the moonlight

Let me dance with St. Francis
and celebrate what remains whole in a damaged world

Pentimento

As I sit in the upper room
    of an Oxford fast food shop
decades of memories parade down
    Corn Market Street
like Mardi Gras dancers in joyous procession
    before the fasting penitential season.

A scholar of image and literary season
    generous in time and found treasure,
A round-faced and red-checked woman
    at a fair with tatting bobbins,
A woman with a black lab
    and an office off High Street,
A young man—those pearls that were his eyes—
    remembered by a black spot beside a waterfall in Ireland.

Following Silver Jubilee markers in the street
    they pass through crowds and time—
pentimento figures among the press and the present.

Fossil

A limestone chert driveway
in rural Blount County
covered in 3-thousand-psi concrete
      with fiber—
350 million years of Alabama history
embedded in obscurity.

Ruffner Mountain

As I stand on this limestone outcrop
looking across the blue-haze valley,
the only sound is the no-sound of wind
more seen in the trees than heard in the ear—
      wind that sailed the Pacific,
      cleared skies over canyons,
      created waves over grain fields,
      blanketed gray-blue these fading fingers of Appalachia,
      to continue eastward across the Atlantic—

I hear you
      in the quiet movement of the trees,
I feel you
      in the journey of the wind—
never silent, never still like the stone
under the brass marker bearing your name.

Marjana Woman's Co-Operative, Morocco

Near Essaouira, oldest in a group of Berber women
seated against the wall of the women's co-op,
she cracked hard-shelled Argan nuts
between stone pestle and rock
in one fluid motion
as smooth as the golden oil that would eventually flow
    from the hand-grinder
at the hand of another.
She caught my eye.

I lifted my camera,
nodding for permission
to capture a moment of her life.
Smiling, she extended her hand,
offering two oval nuts,
our lives conjoining in a flash
of eye-speech and
offering and acceptance.

I did not take the photo.
I have her pictured only in my memory.
But, Belovèd, I saw you in her smile.

Now, in the Argan nuts she placed in my hand
I hold Dame Julian's paradoxical knowing
the size of a hazel nut.

Someday

Someday,
I will have a grand dinner
with the wolf and the subway rider
as guests of honor.

Before the feast,
we shall all
leave a prayer at the banquet wall,
touch our foreheads to the earth,
and bow our heads and
bend our knees,
in reverence to the Belovèd.

World Heritage

On the ridge of Mt. Nebo,
in the shadow of Moses,
I gazed across the Jordan
toward Jerusalem.

In the medieval necropolis
of Chellah, near Rabat,
I stood before the mihrab
of Abu Yusuf's ruined mosque.

At Ephesus in the remains
of the Basilica of St. John,
within sight of the Apostle's tomb,
I descended three steps
into the baptistry's ancient stone pool.

In each, Belovèd,
in each,
feeling the difference between
tourist and pilgrim.

The House of Mary

In Ephesus,
where John found sanctuary
for his given Mother,
sits the House of Mary,
the only woman named in The Qur'an.
High on Mt. Krosessos,
shadowy, squat, and stone,
the oblong room ends in a short
angle to the right, guiding
pilgrims back into the light,
down a descending path to
three fountains—the waters of Mary,
salty waters of healing and blessing—
three arched niches in a prayer wall
covered with scraps of paper and cloth
tied, twisted, pinned,
holding hundreds of prayers and petitions
from all the beloved
rising alike
on the winds of the Aegean.

Mirrored

She was old.
Old at the moment of birth.
Old enough to hold the acorn
   and see the tree.
Old enough to touch a feather
   and feel it in flight.

Old enough to hear the wolf
   and hail the moon.
She was old—
   as only nature can be old.
She was old.

Old enough
   to dissolve into the newness of it all.

Shall We Dance?

Walking the ridge of the mountain,
high among the conifers
the spiced scent of spruce and Christmas in the air,
the Belovèd and I
looked down the valley upon Appalachian hardwoods
swaying in changing weather.
Sourwood and black gum,
tulip trees and thin sassafras
touched tops in undulating waves.
In rising wind, supple spruce
bowed down as though to kiss
oak crowns shifting in time
to alternating gust and breeze.

Moved by the music of it all,
I said,
"My Belovèd! My Belovèd, look
how beautifully the trees waltz to the wind,
as though in rhythm with the whole world!"

The Belovèd smiled, took my hand,
and asked,
"Shall we dance?"

ABOUT THE AUTHOR

Turning attention to writing poetry after over forty years of teaching medieval literature and working in higher education administration, Susan K. Hagen began publishing poems in journals such as *Haiku Journal*, *Ephemerae*, *Cattails*, and *The Avocet: A Journal of Nature Poetry*. Bringing that interest in writing together with her interests in literary gardens of the Middle Ages and horticultural gardens stemming from her work as a Master Gardener, she also launched a blog on gardens and their cultural significance, *After Eden* (aftereden.blog). The site remains active and led to a speaking schedule on gardens, native plants, and pollinators.

Already interested in the writings of the medieval mystics, such as Julian of Norwich, Susan became intrigued with the work of the thirteenth-century Persian poet Rumi during a trip to Turkey in 2014. Soon after, she discovered the work of a next-century Persian poet and mystic, Hafiz. Affinities with these three writers, the English metaphysical poets, and long-lived literary and cultural associations of gardens became the inspiration for *Shall We Dance?*

Susan's academic publications, including *Allegorical Remembrance*, focus on medieval allegory, Geoffrey Chaucer, and Julian of Norwich. She received her undergraduate degree from Gettysburg College, her master's degree from the University of Maryland, and her doctorate in medieval literature from the University of Virginia. She holds the title Mary Collett Munger Professor Emerita of English at Birmingham-Southern College, a private liberal arts college in Alabama. She lives in Birmingham but spends much time at a small lake house where she gardens and finds motivation for her poetry.

ABOUT THE BOOK

This book is set in Garamond Premier Pro, which had its genesis in 1988 when type-designer Robert Slimbach visited the Plantin-Moretus Museum in Antwerp, Belgium, to study its collection of Claude Garamond's metal punches and typefaces. During the fifteen hundreds, Garamond – a Parisian punch-cutter – produced a refined array of book types that combined an unprecedented degree of balance and elegance, for centuries standing as the pinnacle of beauty and practicality in type-founding. Slimbach has created a new interpretation based on Garamond's designs and on compatible italics cut by Robert Granjon, Garamond's contemporary.

Copies of this book can be ordered
from all bookstores including Amazon
and directly from the author,
Susan K. Hagen
4970 Joab Circle
Birmingham, AL 35235.
Please send $17.00 per book
plus $4.00 shipping in AL
and $6.00 beyond AL
by check payable to
Susan K. Hagen.

•

For more information on the work of Susan K. Hagen,
visit http://www.antrimhousebooks.com/authors.html.

www.ingramcontent.com/pod-product-compliance
Lightning Source LLC
Chambersburg PA
CBHW030201100526
44592CB00009B/383